FROM ASPIRING AGENT TO SIX-FIGURE SENSATION

Unveiling the Real Estate Success Formula

Dack Douglas

Icon Publications Limited

CONTENTS

INTRODUCTION

Welcome to a journey that promises to transform your trajectory in the dynamic world of real estate. This book, "From Aspiring Agent to Six-Figure Sensation: Unveiling the Real Estate Success Formula," is your compass to navigate the intricacies of this ever-evolving industry and rise to the coveted ranks of six-figure earners.

Real estate isn't just about properties; it's a realm where your acumen for negotiation, understanding of market trends, and the ability to foster relationships converge to shape your destiny. This book serves as your comprehensive toolkit, meticulously crafted to empower both novices and veterans with the strategies and insights needed to not only navigate but thrive in the bustling real estate arena.

Drawing upon years of experience, industry trends, and success stories, this guide doesn't just offer a list of techniques. It's a holistic approach, designed to cultivate a mindset that fuels growth, resilience, and innovation. From mastering the art of lead generation and honing conversion strategies to leveraging the power of networking and embracing technology, each chapter is meticulously designed to unravel a new facet of your potential.

Whether you're at the threshold of your real estate journey or seeking to transcend income plateaus, "Unleashing Six-Figure Success" is your blueprint for transformation. Prepare to redefine your boundaries and carve your path to financial freedom and professional fulfillment.

The journey to a six-figure income starts here. Are you ready to seize the reins of your destiny? Let's embark on this transformative expedition together.

CHAPTER 1: INTRODUCTION TO REAL ESTATE SUCCESS

Importance Of A Successful Mindset

A successful mindset is crucial for a real estate agent as it shapes their attitude and approach towards their work. It enables them to stay motivated, handle challenges, and adapt to market fluctuations. With a positive and determined mindset, agents can build client trust, negotiate effectively, and consistently pursue opportunities for growth in the competitive real estate industry.

Setting Goals And Objectives

Setting goals and objectives is of paramount importance for real estate agents as it provides a clear roadmap for their professional endeavors. These goals serve as guiding beacons, helping agents focus their efforts, prioritize tasks, and measure their progress. By defining specific targets, agents can enhance their productivity, track achievements, and maintain a proactive approach in meeting client needs, closing deals, and ultimately achieving long-term success in the dynamic realm of real estate.

Overview Of The Real Estate Industry

The real estate industry encompasses a broad spectrum of activities related to the acquisition, sale, and management of properties. It includes residential properties, commercial spaces, industrial sites, and vacant land. Real estate agents play a pivotal role by acting as intermediaries between buyers and sellers. They offer specialized knowledge of the market, guide clients through complex transactions, assess property values, negotiate terms, and ensure adherence to legal procedures. The industry's landscape is influenced by economic conditions, housing demand, interest rates, and regulatory changes, necessitating adaptability and a deep comprehension of market dynamics for success.

The industry's dynamics are influenced by factors such as economic trends, housing demand, interest rates, and local regulations, making it a dynamic and ever-evolving field that demands adaptability and a deep understanding of market nuances.

◆ ◆ ◆

CHAPTER 2: BUILDING A STRONG FOUNDATION

Understanding Real Estate Licensing And Regulations

To understand real estate licensing and regulations, you can start by researching the specific requirements for your region or jurisdiction. This often involves completing pre-licensing education, which may be offered through courses or online programs. Familiarize yourself with the local real estate board or regulatory agency responsible for licensing, as they will provide accurate information about the steps and qualifications needed.

Additionally, attending seminars, workshops, or networking events within the real estate industry can provide insights into current regulations and best practices. Engaging with experienced real estate professionals and mentors can offer valuable guidance and practical knowledge. Staying updated on changes in real estate laws and regulations through industry publications, websites, and official government sources is essential to maintain compliance and ensure a successful real estate career.

Selecting The Right Brokerage

Selecting the right brokerage as a real estate agent involves careful consideration of several factors. Begin by assessing the brokerage's reputation and track record in the industry. Look for a company that aligns with your professional goals and values.

Consider the brokerage's training and support programs, as well as the resources they provide to their agents. A supportive and nurturing environment can greatly contribute to your success.

Evaluate the commission structure, fees, and any contractual obligations. Ensure they are reasonable and fair, allowing you to maximize your earnings.

Meet with current agents at the brokerage to gain insights into their experiences and satisfaction levels. This firsthand perspective can offer valuable information.

Lastly, examine the brokerage's market presence and the areas they specialize in. Choose a brokerage that has a strong presence and expertise in the specific real estate market you intend to work in.

Making an informed decision about the right brokerage will set the foundation for a rewarding and successful real estate career.

Developing Essential Skills: Communication, Negotiation, And Marketing

Developing essential skills as a real estate agent, such as communication, negotiation, and marketing, requires a proactive and structured approach.

For communication, practice active listening and effective verbal and written communication techniques. Engage in role-playing scenarios to enhance your ability to convey information clearly and connect with clients.

To master negotiation, study different negotiation strategies and learn to balance assertiveness with empathy. Seek out opportunities to negotiate in various contexts and reflect on the outcomes to refine your skills.

In the realm of marketing, stay current with digital marketing trends and platforms. Utilize social media, create engaging content, and showcase your listings creatively to attract potential clients.

Continuous learning is essential. Attend workshops, seminars, and industry events focused on these skills. Consider seeking a mentor or coach who can provide personalized guidance and feedback.

Consistent practice, coupled with learning from experiences and seeking feedback, will gradually hone your communication, negotiation, and marketing skills, contributing to your effectiveness and success as a real estate agent.

Communication

Active Listening: Practice active listening by focusing fully on what others are saying without interrupting. This allows you to understand clients' needs and concerns more deeply.

Verbal Communication: Improve your verbal communication by speaking clearly, using appropriate tone and language, and conveying information in a concise and engaging manner.

Nonverbal Communication: Pay attention to your body language, facial expressions, and gestures. Maintain eye contact, use open and inviting gestures, and project confidence.

Empathy: Develop empathy by putting yourself in your clients' shoes and understanding their perspectives. Show genuine care and understanding to build stronger connections.

Clarity and Simplicity: Avoid jargon and technical terms that clients might not understand. Present information in a simple and clear manner to ensure effective communication.

Written Communication: Enhance written communication skills for emails, texts, and marketing materials. Use proper grammar, spelling, and formatting to convey professionalism.

Practice Role-Playing: Engage in role-playing scenarios to simulate client interactions. This helps you refine your responses, address objections, and improve communication under different circumstances.

Feedback and Learning: Seek feedback from colleagues, mentors, or clients to identify areas for improvement. Invest in communication workshops, books, and online courses to enhance your skills.

Adaptability: Tailor your communication style to each client's preferences. Some clients prefer a more formal approach, while others may appreciate a casual and friendly demeanor.

Conflict Resolution: Learn techniques to manage conflicts and difficult conversations professionally. Stay calm, address concerns, and find common ground to reach resolutions.

By consistently practicing these strategies and actively seeking opportunities to communicate effectively, you'll develop strong communication skills that set you apart as a successful real estate agent.

Negotiation

Developing effective negotiation skills as a real estate agent involves a purposeful and gradual process:

Study Negotiation Techniques: Learn about different negotiation strategies, approaches, and tactics through books, courses, and online resources. Understand concepts like win-win outcomes and creating value.

Real-Life Practice: Engage in mock negotiations or role-playing scenarios to simulate real-world situations. Practice with colleagues or mentors to refine your skills and receive constructive feedback.

Observe Experienced Negotiators: Observe experienced real estate agents or other professionals during negotiations. Analyze their techniques, communication styles, and ways they handle challenges.

Active Listening: Pay close attention to your clients' needs, concerns, and preferences. This information can guide your negotiation strategy and help you find mutually beneficial solutions.

Empathy and Building Rapport: Develop empathy to understand your clients' motivations and build rapport. Establishing a strong connection can facilitate smoother negotiations.

Preparation: Thoroughly research the property, market trends, and relevant information before entering negotiations. Being well-prepared enhances your confidence and negotiation position.

Value Proposition: Clearly communicate the value of your offers or proposals to clients. Highlight benefits and advantages that resonate with their interests.

Flexibility: Be adaptable and open to compromise. Understand that negotiations involve give-and-take, and a willingness to adjust your approach can lead to successful outcomes.

Confidence and Poise: Project confidence in your negotiation discussions. Maintain a calm and composed demeanor, even in challenging situations.

Learn from Experiences: Reflect on past negotiations to identify what worked well and areas for improvement. Continuous self-assessment helps refine your approach over time.

Seek Feedback: Request feedback from peers, mentors, or clients who have witnessed your negotiations. Constructive input can help you fine-tune your skills.

By integrating these strategies into your professional practice and consistently seeking opportunities to negotiate, you'll gradually develop effective negotiation skills that contribute to your success as a real estate agent.

Marketing

Developing proficient marketing skills as a real estate agent involves a systematic and hands-on approach:

Market Research: Gain a deep understanding of your local real estate market, including trends, demographics, and competition. This knowledge forms the foundation of effective marketing strategies.

Digital Proficiency: Familiarize yourself with digital marketing tools and platforms. Create and maintain a professional online presence through social media, websites, and listing platforms.

Content Creation: Develop high-quality content that showcases your expertise and properties. Create engaging videos, blog posts, and visual materials to attract and educate potential clients.

Target Audience: Define your target audience and tailor your marketing efforts to their preferences and needs. Personalized marketing resonates more effectively with potential clients.

Branding: Establish a distinct brand identity that reflects your values and style. Consistent branding across all marketing materials enhances recognition and credibility.

Networking: Build relationships with local professionals, including other agents, lenders, and contractors. Networking can lead to collaborative marketing opportunities and referrals.

Client Testimonials: Collect and showcase positive testimonials from satisfied clients. Authentic feedback boosts your credibility and reinforces your marketing efforts.

Visual Appeal: Invest in high-quality property photography and staging. Visually appealing content can significantly impact potential buyers' and sellers' perceptions.

Analytical Skills: Learn to interpret marketing analytics to gauge the effectiveness of your strategies. Adjust your approach based on data-driven insights for optimal results.

Continuous Learning: Stay updated on marketing trends, techniques, and tools. Attend workshops, webinars, and courses to refine your skills and adapt to evolving industry practices.

Innovative Approaches: Experiment with innovative marketing methods, such as virtual tours, 3D walkthroughs, or interactive content, to engage clients in unique ways.

By implementing these strategies consistently and adapting them to your market and client preferences, you'll progressively enhance your marketing skills and establish a strong presence in the competitive real estate landscape.

◆ ◆ ◆

CHAPTER 3: MASTERING MARKET KNOWLEDGE

Conducting Local Market Research

Conducting effective local market research as a real estate agent involves a systematic and thorough approach:

Data Collection: Gather relevant data on property sales, listings, and market trends in your target area. Utilize real estate databases, local property records, and reputable online platforms.

Market Reports: Access market reports provided by local real estate associations or industry experts. These reports offer valuable insights into pricing trends, inventory levels, and demand.

Neighborhood Analysis: Study specific neighborhoods within your market. Evaluate factors like property types, amenities, schools, crime rates, and proximity to key attractions.

Comparable Sales: Analyze recent comparable sales (comps) to understand property values and pricing dynamics. Compare similar properties to determine fair market values.

Supply and Demand: Assess supply and demand dynamics by tracking the number of active listings and sales over time. Identify patterns that can help you anticipate market shifts.

Economic Indicators: Consider local economic indicators like employment rates, population growth, and major infrastructure projects. These factors influence the overall real estate market.

Local Regulations: Stay informed about zoning regulations, development plans, and any legal restrictions that may impact property transactions or values.

Networking: Establish connections with local appraisers, fellow agents, lenders, and other industry professionals. Their insights and perspectives can provide valuable market intelligence.

Consumer Behavior: Understand buyer and seller behavior in your market. Identify preferences, motivations, and trends that can guide your marketing and client interactions.

Online Tools: Utilize online tools and platforms that offer market insights, such as demographic data, crime statistics, and school ratings, to enhance your research.

Community Involvement: Participate in community events, attend local meetings, and engage with residents to gain firsthand knowledge of the area's culture and dynamics.

Continuous Learning: Stay updated on changes in the local market by regularly reviewing news articles, attending real estate seminars, and joining relevant forums or groups.

By diligently applying these strategies and continuously refining your local market research skills, you'll be better equipped to provide accurate and valuable guidance to your clients as a knowledgeable real estate agent.

Staying Updated With Market Trends

Staying updated with market trends as a real estate agent requires a proactive and multifaceted approach:

Industry Publications: Regularly read industry-specific publications, magazines, and websites that offer insights into current real estate market conditions, emerging trends, and expert opinions.

Local News: Stay informed about local news and economic developments that could impact the real estate market, such as infrastructure projects, zoning changes, or new businesses opening.

Real Estate Associations: Join local and national real estate associations, which often provide market reports, statistics, and research to members. Attend their events to connect with fellow professionals and access valuable information.

Market Reports: Leverage market reports and analysis provided by reputable real estate research firms or consulting agencies. These reports often offer data-driven insights into market trends and forecasts.

Networking: Establish a strong network of industry professionals, including fellow agents, brokers, appraisers, and lenders. Regular conversations with peers can provide firsthand information about shifts in the market.

Social Media: Follow influential real estate professionals, economists, and industry thought leaders on social media platforms. Their posts and updates can offer timely insights into market dynamics.

Webinars and Workshops: Participate in webinars, workshops, and seminars focused on real estate trends and market analysis. These events provide opportunities to learn from experts and ask questions.

Local Experts: Build relationships with local economists, researchers, and analysts who specialize in real estate or the local economy. Their expertise can provide valuable context for market trends.

Property Listings: Regularly review property listings to gauge pricing trends and inventory levels. This hands-on approach can help you spot changes and shifts in the market.

Data Analysis: Utilize real estate databases and market analytics tools to track historical data, identify patterns, and make informed projections about market trends.

Continuous Learning: Embrace a mindset of continuous learning and curiosity. The real estate industry evolves, so staying curious and open to new information is essential.

By combining these strategies and dedicating time to staying informed, you'll be well-equipped to navigate shifts in the real estate market and provide valuable insights to your clients.

Analyzing Property Values And Pricing Strategies

Analyzing property values and formulating effective pricing strategies as a real estate agent involves a systematic and informed approach:

Comparable Sales (Comps): Research recently sold properties that are similar to the one you're analyzing in terms of location, size, features, and condition. Compare these comps to derive a preliminary value estimate.

Market Trends: Stay abreast of current market trends, including supply and demand dynamics, to gauge the overall climate and potential impacts on property values.

Neighborhood Factors: Consider the influence of the property's neighborhood, amenities, schools, crime rates, and proximity to essential services. These factors contribute to its value.

Property Condition: Assess the property's condition, age, and any necessary repairs or renovations. Adjust the value estimate based on its state of maintenance.

Local Appraisers: Consult local appraisers to gain insights into property values and appraisal methodologies commonly used in the area.

Property Features: Evaluate unique features, upgrades, and special characteristics of the property that could positively or negatively affect its value compared to similar properties.

Seller's Motivation: Understand the seller's motivations, such as urgency to sell or willingness to negotiate. Align the pricing strategy with the seller's objectives.

Competitor Analysis: Analyze active listings in the market to understand the competition. Determine how the property stacks up against similar listings and adjust the pricing strategy accordingly.

Historical Data: Review historical sales data to identify price trends and cycles in the area. This can provide insights into potential future value changes.

Pricing Psychology: Consider the psychological aspects of pricing, such as pricing just below a round number to create the perception of a better deal.

Feedback and Testing: Gather feedback from potential buyers who have viewed the property. Adjust the pricing strategy based on their reactions and level of interest.

Flexibility: Be prepared to adjust the pricing strategy if the property doesn't attract interest within a reasonable timeframe. Market conditions may warrant reevaluation.

By blending these approaches and adapting them to the specific property and market conditions, you'll be better equipped to accurately analyze property values and devise effective pricing strategies that align with both market dynamics and client objectives.

❖ ❖ ❖

CHAPTER 4: EFFECTIVE LEAD GENERATION

Prospecting For Clients: Strategies And Techniques

Prospecting for clients as a real estate agent involves a mix of proactive approaches and relationship-building techniques:

Networking Events: Attend local networking events, business mixers, and community gatherings to connect with potential clients and fellow professionals.

Referrals: Cultivate relationships with past clients, colleagues, and friends who can refer potential clients to you based on their positive experiences.

Online Presence: Establish a strong online presence through a professional website, social media profiles, and engaging content that showcases your expertise.

Cold Calling: Reach out to potential clients through cold calls, introducing yourself and offering your services with a focus on how you can address their needs.

Direct Mail: Send targeted direct mail campaigns, such as postcards or newsletters, to specific neighborhoods or demographics to create awareness.

Open Houses: Host open houses to meet potential buyers and sellers while showcasing your knowledge of properties and the local market.

Farm Areas: Concentrate your efforts in specific neighborhoods, becoming a local expert and consistently engaging with residents through events or newsletters.

Door Knocking: Personally visit homes in targeted areas to introduce yourself, provide market information, and offer your assistance.

Social Media Marketing: Utilize social media platforms to share property listings, market updates, and informative content that resonates with potential clients.

Partnerships: Collaborate with local businesses like mortgage brokers, interior designers, or contractors for mutually beneficial referrals.

Seminars and Workshops: Organize or participate in seminars or workshops on real estate topics, positioning yourself as a knowledgeable resource.

Lead Generation Tools: Utilize lead generation tools, CRM software, and online platforms to capture and nurture leads effectively.

Client Testimonials: Showcase positive client testimonials and reviews on your marketing materials and online platforms to build credibility.

Offer Free Resources: Provide valuable resources like market reports, buying/selling guides, or investment tips to attract and engage potential clients.

By adopting a combination of these strategies and tailoring them to your strengths and market, you'll create a well-rounded prospecting approach that helps you connect with potential clients and expand your real estate business.

Tilizing Online And Offline Marketing Channels

Utilizing both online and offline marketing channels effectively as a real estate agent involves a balanced and integrated approach:

Online Marketing:

Professional Website: Create a user-friendly website showcasing your services, listings, and market insights. Ensure it's mobile-responsive and optimized for search engines.

Social Media Presence: Establish active profiles on platforms like Facebook, Instagram, and LinkedIn. Share engaging content, property listings, and informative posts to connect with a wider audience.

Digital Advertising: Invest in targeted online ads on platforms such as Google Ads or social media to reach potential clients based on demographics and interests.

Email Marketing: Build a subscriber list and send regular newsletters containing market updates, property highlights, and valuable insights to stay connected with leads.

Virtual Tours: Utilize virtual tours and 3D walkthroughs to showcase properties online, providing a comprehensive view to potential buyers.

Blogging and Content: Maintain a blog where you publish informative articles about the real estate market, buying/selling tips, and local insights to establish authority.

Online Reviews: Encourage satisfied clients to leave positive reviews on platforms like Google or Yelp, enhancing your online reputation.

Offline Marketing:

Print Marketing: Design and distribute brochures, flyers, and postcards highlighting your services and properties in key locations.

Direct Mail: Send targeted direct mail campaigns to specific neighborhoods, introducing yourself and your offerings.

Local Events: Participate in community events, trade shows, and local fairs to interact with potential clients face-to-face.

Networking: Attend industry events, seminars, and local business gatherings to establish relationships with fellow professionals and potential clients.

Open Houses: Host engaging open houses to provide a firsthand experience of properties and connect with potential buyers.

Billboards and Signage: Use strategically placed billboards and signage to increase visibility in high-traffic areas.

Referral Programs: Develop referral programs with local businesses, offering incentives for referrals that lead to successful transactions.

Print Advertising: Place ads in local newspapers, magazines, or real estate publications to reach a wider offline audience.

By combining these online and offline strategies, you'll create a comprehensive marketing approach that maximizes your reach and engages potential clients through various channels, ultimately contributing to your success as a real estate agent.

Building And Nurturing A Referral Network

Building and nurturing a referral network as a real estate agent involves strategic relationship-building and consistent efforts:

Client Satisfaction: Prioritize exceptional service to your current clients. A satisfied client is more likely to refer friends, family, and colleagues to you.

Stay in Touch: Maintain regular communication with past clients through personalized emails, newsletters, or occasional phone calls. Share market updates and valuable information.

Networking Events: Attend local networking events, industry gatherings, and community functions to connect with fellow professionals and potential referral partners.

Mutually Beneficial Partnerships: Collaborate with mortgage brokers, attorneys, contractors, and other related professionals. Establish partnerships where referrals can flow both ways.

Express Gratitude: Send personalized thank-you notes or small tokens of appreciation to clients who refer business your way. Expressing gratitude strengthens relationships.

Social Media Engagement: Engage with your social media followers by responding to comments, sharing valuable content, and participating in conversations to foster connections.

Referral Programs: Create a structured referral program that rewards clients and partners for successful referrals, incentivizing them to actively recommend your services.

Educational Workshops: Organize workshops or seminars on relevant real estate topics. Sharing knowledge enhances your reputation and attracts referrals.

Regular Follow-ups: Keep in touch with potential referral sources through periodic emails, updates, or meetings to stay top-of-mind when opportunities arise.

Offer Value: Continuously provide value to your referral network by sharing market insights, industry trends, and educational resources.

Personalized Interactions: Tailor your interactions to each individual's preferences and needs. Personalized communication strengthens relationships.

Consistency: Consistently nurture your referral network over time. Building trust and rapport requires ongoing effort and genuine engagement.

By consistently applying these strategies, you'll develop a strong referral network that generates a steady stream of qualified leads and reinforces your reputation as a trustworthy and reliable real estate agent.

◆ ◆ ◆

CHAPTER 5: SUCCESSFUL LISTING AND PRESENTATION

Crafting Compelling Property Listings

Crafting compelling property listings as a real estate agent involves a blend of creativity, clarity, and attention to detail:

Engaging Headlines: Start with a captivating headline that highlights the property's unique features or benefits to capture potential buyers' attention.

Clear Descriptions: Write concise and descriptive property descriptions, focusing on key selling points such as location, amenities, and notable features.

Emotional Appeal: Evoke emotions by describing how the property could enhance the buyer's lifestyle. Paint a vivid picture of how they could envision themselves living there.

Highlight Features: Showcase standout features like updated appliances, spacious layouts, scenic views, or proximity to attractions.

Use Visuals: Include high-quality photos that showcase the property from various angles and capture its best attributes. Virtual tours or videos can offer immersive experiences.

Specific Details: Provide specific details such as square footage, number of bedrooms and bathrooms, and any recent renovations or upgrades.

Neighborhood Insights: Describe the neighborhood's appeal, mentioning nearby schools, parks, shopping, and dining options.

Call to Action: Encourage potential buyers to take action by inviting them to schedule a showing or contact you for more information.

Storytelling: Share a brief story or anecdote about the property's history or its previous occupants to create a personal connection.

Highlight Value: Clearly communicate the value proposition, whether it's an investment opportunity, a move-in-ready home, or potential for customization.

Error-Free Writing: Ensure your listing is free of grammatical errors and typos to maintain a professional image.

Keywords and SEO: Incorporate relevant keywords and phrases that potential buyers might use in their online searches to improve the listing's visibility.

Honesty and Transparency: Provide accurate and truthful information, avoiding exaggerations or misleading statements that could erode trust.

By combining these elements, you'll create property listings that not only inform potential buyers but also ignite their interest and imagination, increasing the likelihood of inquiries and showings.

Presenting Properties To Clients Effectively

Presenting properties to clients effectively as a real estate agent involves a strategic and client-focused approach:

Preparation: Thoroughly research and familiarize yourself with the property's details, history, and neighborhood before the presentation.

Personalization: Tailor your presentation to the client's preferences and needs, highlighting features that align with their requirements.

Visual Aids: Utilize high-quality photos, virtual tours, and videos to provide a comprehensive view of the property, enhancing the client's understanding.

Key Selling Points: Emphasize the property's standout features, such as updated amenities, unique architectural elements, or potential for customization.

Neighborhood Insights: Provide information about the surrounding area, including schools, parks, transportation, and local amenities.

Comparative Analysis: Share recent sales data and comparable properties to justify the property's value and pricing.

Address Concerns: Anticipate and address potential questions or concerns the client might have during the presentation.

Storytelling: Share engaging stories about the property's history, previous occupants, or memorable events to create an emotional connection.

Open Dialogue: Encourage clients to ask questions and express their thoughts during the presentation, fostering an interactive and informative discussion.

Timing and Pace: Deliver information at a comfortable pace, allowing clients to absorb details without feeling rushed.

Room-by-Room Tour: Guide clients through each room, highlighting the functionality and unique aspects of each space.

Allow Exploration: Give clients time to explore the property on their own, allowing them to visualize themselves living in the space.

Follow-Up: After the presentation, follow up with additional materials, such as property brochures or digital resources, to reinforce the information shared.

Feedback and Flexibility: Solicit feedback on the presentation and property tour, and be open to adjusting your approach based on client preferences.

By combining these strategies, you'll create property presentations that effectively engage clients, provide comprehensive information, and empower them to make informed decisions.

Showcasing The Unique Selling Points Of Listings

Effectively showcasing the unique selling points of listings as a real estate agent involves a strategic and client-focused approach:

Prioritize Features: Identify the property's standout features, whether it's a stunning view, modern upgrades, spacious layout, or unique architectural elements.

Compelling Descriptions: Craft descriptive and engaging narratives that vividly depict how these features enhance the property's appeal and potential.

Visual Impact: Use high-quality, professional photos that highlight the unique features and create an emotional connection with potential buyers.

Virtual Tours: Provide interactive virtual tours or videos that allow clients to experience the property's unique attributes firsthand.

Neighborhood Context: Illustrate how the property's unique features integrate with the neighborhood's offerings, such as nearby parks, schools, or entertainment.

Storytelling: Share anecdotes or stories that showcase how previous occupants have enjoyed or benefited from the property's distinctive aspects.

Comparative Analysis: Compare the property's unique features to similar listings in the area, demonstrating its added value.

Customization Potential: Highlight opportunities for personalization or expansion that make the property especially appealing to potential buyers.

Practical Benefits: Emphasize how the unique features contribute to practical benefits, such as energy efficiency, low maintenance, or improved quality of life.

Client-Centric Approach: Tailor your presentation of unique selling points based on the client's preferences and priorities.

Open Discussion: Encourage clients to share their thoughts and reactions to the property's unique features, fostering an interactive and informative conversation.

Supporting Materials: Provide additional materials, such as brochures or fact sheets, that reinforce the property's unique attributes.

Expert Insights: Offer your professional insights on how the property's unique features align with current market trends and buyer preferences.

By integrating these strategies, you'll effectively showcase the unique selling points of your listings, capturing the attention and imagination of potential buyers and highlighting the distinct advantages of each property.

◆ ◆ ◆

CHAPTER 6: THE ART OF NEGOTIATION

Strategies For Successful Negotiations

Achieving successful negotiations as a real estate agent involves a skillful and strategic approach:

Active Listening: Pay close attention to the other party's needs, preferences, and concerns. Listen actively to gather valuable insights that can guide your negotiation strategy.

Empathy and Understanding: Put yourself in the other party's shoes to understand their motivations and create a more collaborative atmosphere.

Effective Communication: Clearly and confidently articulate your client's position, emphasizing the property's strengths and value while addressing any potential objections.

Build Rapport: Establish a positive rapport with the other party through genuine interactions and respectful communication.

Preparation: Thoroughly research the property, market conditions, and relevant data to bolster your negotiation position with informed insights.

Win-Win Mindset: Aim for mutually beneficial outcomes that address the interests of both parties, fostering goodwill and increasing the likelihood of agreement.

Flexibility: Be open to creative solutions and alternative approaches that meet the needs of all parties involved.

Timing: Choose the right timing for negotiations, considering factors like market conditions, property demand, and the other party's circumstances.

Use of Silence: Employ strategic pauses during negotiations to encourage the other party to share additional information or make concessions.

Stay Calm: Maintain a composed and professional demeanor even in challenging moments, projecting confidence and credibility.

Leverage Information: Utilize market data, comparable sales, and relevant information to support your arguments and substantiate your client's position.

Exploring Trade-Offs: Identify potential trade-offs or concessions that can help bridge gaps and facilitate agreement.

Third-Party Mediation: If negotiations become contentious, consider involving a neutral third party, such as a mediator or attorney, to facilitate a resolution.

Document Agreements: Clearly document any agreements, terms, or concessions in writing to avoid misunderstandings and ensure a smooth transaction.

By employing these negotiation strategies, you'll enhance your ability to navigate real estate negotiations effectively, securing favorable outcomes for your clients while maintaining professionalism and building positive relationships.

Handling Offers And Counteroffers

Handling offers and counter-offers as a real estate agent requires a strategic and responsive approach:

Prompt Communication: Respond to offers and counter-offers promptly to demonstrate your commitment and maintain the momentum of negotiations.

Analyze Terms: Carefully review the terms of each offer or counter-offer, considering not only the price but also contingencies, timelines, and other relevant factors.

Consult with Clients: Consult your clients to understand their priorities and preferences, helping you craft a strategic response that aligns with their goals.

Counter with Clarity: Craft counter-offers with clear and specific terms, outlining any modifications or adjustments to the original proposal.

Negotiate Respectfully: Maintain a respectful and professional tone in all communications, fostering a positive and collaborative negotiation environment.

Leverage Market Insights: Use relevant market data, comparable sales, and local trends to support your counter-offer and substantiate your client's position.

Emphasize Value: Highlight the value of your client's property and address any concerns raised by the other party in your counter-offer.

Consider Timing: Factor in the timing of the offer or counter-offer in relation to market conditions, property demand, and your client's priorities.

Stay Open to Dialogue: Keep the lines of communication open and be willing to engage in back-and-forth discussions to reach a mutually acceptable agreement.

Alternative Scenarios: Present alternative scenarios or options to the other party that could lead to a compromise and successful resolution.

Third-Party Mediation: If negotiations reach an impasse, consider involving a neutral third party, such as a mediator or attorney, to facilitate productive discussions.

Document Agreements: Once an offer is accepted or a counter-offer is agreed upon, ensure that all terms are accurately documented in writing to avoid misunderstandings.

Client's Best Interests: Continuously advocate for your client's best interests while exploring opportunities for a mutually beneficial outcome.

By applying these strategies, you'll adeptly navigate the offer and counter-offer process, ensuring effective communication, strategic negotiations, and successful outcomes for your clients in the real estate transaction.

Closing Deals And Managing Client Expectations

Closing deals and managing client expectations as a real estate agent requires a balanced and proactive approach:

Clear Communication: Maintain transparent and consistent communication with clients throughout the closing process, ensuring they are well-informed and aware of each step.

Educate Clients: Provide thorough explanations of the closing process, legal requirements, and potential challenges to help clients anticipate and understand what to expect.

Set Realistic Expectations: Set achievable expectations from the outset, outlining potential timelines, market conditions, and possible outcomes to prevent unrealistic assumptions.

Detailed Timelines: Create a detailed timeline that outlines key milestones and deadlines, helping clients visualize the progression toward closing.

Regular Updates: Keep clients updated on the status of the transaction, addressing any concerns promptly and providing reassurance.

Problem Solving: Anticipate and address potential issues that may arise during closing, presenting solutions and guiding clients through any obstacles.

Collaborative Approach: Involve clients in decision-making processes, encouraging their active participation and making them feel empowered and in control.

Manage Emotions: Recognize that buying or selling real estate can be emotional. Acknowledge and empathize with clients' feelings while providing practical guidance.

Legal Expertise: Collaborate with legal professionals to ensure all legal aspects of the transaction are accurately handled and explained to clients.

Thorough Documentation: Ensure all required documentation is accurately completed and submitted in a timely manner, minimizing delays and potential complications.

Final Walk-Through: Arrange and guide clients through a final walk-through of the property before closing to address any last-minute concerns.

Closing Preparation: Assist clients in preparing for the closing day by providing details about the location, necessary documents, and any additional steps.

Celebrate Achievements: Acknowledge milestones and achievements throughout the closing process, reinforcing the positive aspects of the transaction.

Post-Closing Follow-Up: Stay engaged even after the deal is closed, following up to ensure client satisfaction and addressing any lingering questions or concerns.

By embracing these strategies, you'll adeptly navigate the closing process, effectively manage client expectations, and ensure a smooth and satisfying experience for both buyers and sellers in the real estate transaction.

❖ ❖ ❖

CHAPTER 7: PROVIDING EXCEPTIONAL CLIENT SERVICE

Building Strong Client Relationships

Building strong client relationships as a real estate agent requires a personalized and client-centered approach:

Effective Communication: Maintain open and timely communication with clients, actively listening to their needs, concerns, and preferences.

Trust and Transparency: Foster trust by being transparent about market conditions, property details, and potential challenges throughout the process.

Personalized Approach: Tailor your services to each client's unique circumstances, preferences, and goals, showing that their needs are your top priority.

Regular Updates: Keep clients informed about market trends, property showings, and transaction progress, demonstrating your commitment to their success.

Educational Guidance: Provide educational resources and explanations about the buying or selling process, empowering clients to make informed decisions.

Responsive Availability: Be accessible and responsive to client inquiries and concerns, showing that you're dedicated to providing exceptional service.

Professionalism: Conduct yourself with professionalism, integrity, and a client-focused attitude in all interactions.

Empathy and Understanding: Understand and acknowledge the emotional aspects of real estate transactions, offering empathy and support during stressful moments.

Personal Connection: Build rapport by showing genuine interest in your clients' lives and aspirations, creating a stronger and more meaningful relationship.

Exceed Expectations: Go above and beyond to exceed client expectations, whether it's providing extra market research, organizing property tours, or offering helpful insights.

Post-Transaction Engagement: Maintain contact after the transaction is complete, sending follow-up messages, anniversary greetings, or market updates to stay connected.

Feedback Loop: Encourage clients to share feedback and testimonials, showcasing your commitment to continuous improvement and client satisfaction.

Client Appreciation: Express gratitude for their business through personalized gestures such as handwritten notes, small gifts, or invitations to client appreciation events.

Consistent Care: Whether it's a small question or a major decision, consistently show that you're dedicated to supporting your clients' real estate journey.

By embracing these strategies, you'll establish strong and lasting client relationships that not only lead to successful transactions but also foster trust, loyalty, and positive referrals in your real estate career.

Delivering Outstanding Customer Service

Delivering outstanding customer service as a real estate agent requires a proactive and client-centered approach:

Client-Centric Attitude: Place your clients' needs, preferences, and goals at the forefront of every interaction, showing that their satisfaction is your priority.

Effective Communication: Maintain clear and consistent communication throughout the entire process, keeping clients informed and engaged.

Timely Responsiveness: Respond promptly to calls, emails, and inquiries, demonstrating your commitment to addressing client concerns promptly.

Attentive Listening: Actively listen to your clients to understand their specific requirements, concerns, and aspirations, tailoring your services accordingly.

Educational Support: Provide comprehensive information about market trends, property details, and transaction steps, empowering clients to make informed decisions.

Expertise and Guidance: Offer your expert insights and guidance, helping clients navigate complex real estate transactions with confidence.

Problem-Solving: Anticipate challenges and proactively offer solutions to mitigate issues that may arise during the buying or selling process.

Flexibility and Adaptability: Adjust your approach to suit each client's unique situation, preferences, and timeline, ensuring a personalized experience.

Professional Integrity: Conduct yourself with honesty, transparency, and ethical behavior, earning clients' trust and confidence in your services.

Above-and-Beyond Efforts: Go the extra mile by offering additional research, personalized property tours, or assistance with related services like mortgage referrals.

Emotional Support: Recognize that real estate transactions can be emotionally charged; provide empathy and understanding during challenging moments.

Post-Transaction Care: Maintain contact after the transaction is complete, providing continued assistance, market updates, and resources.

Feedback and Improvement: Encourage clients to provide feedback and actively seek ways to improve your services based on their input.

Client Satisfaction Surveys: Consider sending satisfaction surveys to gauge client experiences and identify areas for enhancement.

By embracing these principles, you'll consistently deliver exceptional customer service that not only meets but surpasses client expectations, fostering positive relationships and establishing a reputation as a trusted and reliable real estate professional.

Managing Client Feedback And Concerns

Effectively managing client feedback and concerns as a real estate agent requires a responsive and client-centered approach:

Open Communication: Create an environment where clients feel comfortable sharing their feedback and concerns, promoting open and honest discussions.

Active Listening: Listen attentively to understand the nature of their feedback or concern, demonstrating empathy and genuine interest.

Prompt Response: Address client feedback and concerns promptly, showing your commitment to resolving issues in a timely manner.

Validation and Empathy: Acknowledge their feelings and perspectives, showing empathy and understanding for their point of view.

Investigation: Thoroughly investigate the issue or concern to gather relevant information and assess the situation from all angles.

Transparent Explanation: Provide a clear and transparent explanation of the situation, sharing relevant details and potential solutions.

Problem-Solving: Collaborate with clients to explore possible solutions and alternatives, working together to find a resolution that aligns with their goals.

Regular Updates: Keep clients informed of the progress and steps taken to address their concern, ensuring they remain engaged in the resolution process.

Escalation Plan: If the concern is complex, have a plan in place to escalate the matter to higher levels of authority or involve relevant professionals.

Client-Centered Resolution: Prioritize solutions that align with the client's best interests, even if it involves additional effort on your part.

Learning Opportunity: Use feedback and concerns as opportunities for growth and improvement, adapting your approach to prevent similar issues in the future.

Follow-Up: After a concern is resolved, follow up with clients to ensure their satisfaction and gather feedback on the effectiveness of the resolution.

Documentation: Keep detailed records of client feedback, concerns, and the steps taken to address them for future reference.

Continuous Improvement: Continuously refine your practices based on client feedback, aiming to enhance your services and overall client experience.

By adopting these strategies, you'll not only effectively manage client feedback and concerns but also reinforce your commitment to delivering exceptional service and maintaining positive client relationships in the real estate industry.

◆ ◆ ◆

CHAPTER 8: LEVERAGING TECHNOLOGY AND TOOLS

Using Real Estate Software And CRM Systems

When it comes to real estate software and CRM systems, selecting the right tools can greatly enhance your efficiency and client management. Consider integrating the following options into your workflow:

Customer Relationship Management (CRM) Systems: CRMs like Salesforce, HubSpot, or Zoho CRM help you organize client information, track interactions, and manage leads effectively.

Property Listing Platforms: Utilize platforms like Zillow, Realtor.com, or MLS to list and showcase properties, reaching a broader audience of potential buyers.

Virtual Tour and 3D Software: Tools like Matterport or EyeSpy360 enable you to create virtual property tours, enhancing the online viewing experience for clients.

Document Management: Services like DocuSign or Dotloop streamline the process of signing and managing contracts, making transactions more efficient.

Market Analysis and Data Tools: Platforms such as CoreLogic, Reonomy, or Realist provide valuable market insights, helping you analyze property values and trends.

Email Marketing: Tools like Mailchimp or Constant Contact assist in creating and sending targeted email campaigns to stay engaged with clients.

Social Media Management: Software like Buffer or Hootsuite help schedule and manage your social media posts, maintaining an active online presence.

Accounting and Financial Tools: QuickBooks or Xero help you manage your finances, track expenses, and maintain accurate records.

Project Management Tools: Tools like Trello or Asana can help you stay organized, manage tasks, and collaborate effectively with clients and team members.

Mobile Apps: Consider real estate apps like Homesnap, Redfin, or Zillow for on-the-go property searches and market insights.

Analytics and Reporting: Google Analytics or HubSpot Analytics can help you track website performance and marketing efforts.

Client Communication: Utilize tools like Slack or Microsoft Teams for seamless communication and collaboration with clients and team members.

When choosing software and CRM systems, assess your specific needs, budget, and the scalability of the tools. Integration and ease of use are also crucial factors to ensure a streamlined and efficient real estate operation.

Harnessing Social Media For Marketing

Harnessing social media for marketing as a real estate agent involves a strategic and engaging approach:

Platform Selection: Identify the social media platforms that align with your target audience. Facebook, Instagram, LinkedIn, and Twitter are popular choices for real estate professionals.

Content Strategy: Develop a content strategy that balances property listings, market insights, informative articles, and engaging visuals to showcase your expertise.

Visual Appeal: Use high-quality photos and videos to showcase properties, emphasizing their unique features and creating an emotional connection with potential buyers.

Consistent Posting: Maintain a regular posting schedule to keep your audience engaged and informed. Consistency helps build your online presence.

Engagement: Interact with your audience by responding to comments, messages, and inquiries promptly. Foster conversations to create a sense of community.

Hashtags: Utilize relevant hashtags to increase the visibility of your posts and reach a broader audience interested in real estate.

Local Insights: Share insights about local neighborhoods, schools, amenities, and events to position yourself as a knowledgeable local expert.

Virtual Tours: Leverage live video or virtual tour features to conduct property walkthroughs and engage with potential buyers in real-time.

Client Stories: Highlight success stories, testimonials, or case studies from satisfied clients to build trust and credibility.

Educational Content: Provide educational content about the real estate process, market trends, buying/selling tips, and investment strategies.

Collaborations: Partner with local businesses, interior designers, or mortgage brokers for joint promotions or cross-promotions to expand your reach.

Paid Advertising: Consider running targeted social media ads to reach specific demographics and promote your listings or services.

Community Engagement: Participate in local groups, forums, or events to connect with potential clients and establish your presence within the community.

Analytics and Insights: Regularly analyze your social media metrics to understand which content resonates best with your audience and make data-driven adjustments.

By integrating these strategies, you'll effectively leverage social media to showcase properties, provide valuable insights, and connect with potential clients, ultimately enhancing your real estate marketing efforts.

Incorporating Virtual Tours And Digital Marketing Strategies

Incorporating virtual tools into digital marketing strategies as a real estate agent can significantly enhance your reach and engagement:

Virtual Tours and Videos: Create immersive virtual property tours and videos that allow potential buyers to explore homes online, providing a realistic viewing experience.

Live Streaming: Utilize live streaming on platforms like Facebook or Instagram to conduct virtual open houses, Q&A sessions, or property tours in real-time.

Interactive Floor Plans: Offer interactive floor plans that allow users to visualize the layout and flow of a property, enhancing their understanding.

Augmented Reality (AR): Implement AR tools that enable clients to virtually stage or customize spaces, helping them envision the property's potential.

360-Degree Photos: Use 360-degree photos to capture comprehensive views of interiors and exteriors, allowing viewers to virtually navigate through spaces.

Digital Signatures: Incorporate digital signature solutions to streamline the signing of contracts and documents, enhancing the efficiency of transactions.

Online Workshops or Webinars: Host webinars or workshops that offer insights into the real estate market, home buying/selling process, and investment strategies.

AI-Powered Chatbots: Implement AI-powered chatbots on your website or social media to provide instant responses to inquiries and engage with visitors.

Virtual Reality (VR): Integrate VR technology for a fully immersive experience, enabling clients to virtually "walk through" properties from anywhere.

Targeted Online Ads: Utilize targeted online ads to promote virtual property tours, reaching specific demographics interested in real estate.

Engagement and Gamification: Use interactive elements or gamification techniques to engage users during virtual property tours or online events.

Content Diversification: Mix virtual tools with a variety of content, such as blog posts, infographics, and market reports, to offer a comprehensive digital experience.

Client Portals: Create secure online portals where clients can access personalized property listings, documents, and updates in one centralized location.

Feedback and Analytics: Collect user feedback and analyze digital engagement metrics to refine your virtual tools and tailor your strategies over time.

By integrating these virtual tools into your digital marketing strategies, you'll enhance the online experience for potential buyers and sellers, showcase properties more effectively, and establish yourself as a tech-savvy and forward-thinking real estate agent.

◆ ◆ ◆

CHAPTER 9: SCALING YOUR REAL ESTATE BUSINESS

Hiring And Managing A Real Estate Team

Hiring and managing a real estate team requires careful planning and effective leadership:

Clear Vision and Roles: Define your team's mission, goals, and individual roles to ensure everyone understands their responsibilities and contributes to the collective success.

Recruitment Strategy: Identify the skills and qualities you seek in team members and conduct thorough interviews to select individuals who align with your vision.

Effective Training: Provide comprehensive onboarding and ongoing training to equip team members with the necessary skills and knowledge for their roles.

Open Communication: Foster transparent communication within the team, encouraging open dialogue, feedback, and collaboration to address challenges and promote innovation.

Lead by Example: Set a strong example by demonstrating professionalism, work ethic, and dedication, inspiring your team to emulate these qualities.

Delegate Wisely: Delegate tasks based on team members' strengths and expertise, empowering them to take ownership of their responsibilities.

Motivation and Recognition: Recognize and reward team members' achievements, whether through incentives, praise, or growth opportunities, to maintain morale and motivation.

Goal Setting: Establish clear performance goals and benchmarks for the team and individuals, tracking progress and celebrating milestones together.

Problem Solving: Encourage a problem-solving mindset within the team, facilitating brainstorming sessions and collaborative approaches to overcome challenges.

Respect Diversity: Value and respect the diverse perspectives and strengths that each team member brings, fostering an inclusive and dynamic environment.

Conflict Resolution: Address conflicts or disagreements promptly and professionally, mediating discussions to ensure a harmonious work environment.

Empowerment: Empower team members to make decisions within their roles, promoting autonomy and accountability for their contributions.

Continuous Learning: Invest in ongoing professional development opportunities, workshops, and industry updates to keep the team's skills and knowledge current.

Flexible Leadership: Adapt your leadership style to the individual needs and preferences of your team members, cultivating a culture of trust and mutual respect.

By implementing these strategies, you'll establish a cohesive and productive real estate team that collaborates effectively, achieves shared goals, and contributes to your overall success as a leader in the industry.

Expanding Your Client Base And Geographic Reach

Expanding your client base and geographic reach as a real estate agent involves a strategic and proactive approach:

Targeted Marketing: Develop a comprehensive marketing plan that includes digital advertising, social media campaigns, and traditional methods to reach a wider audience.

Local Networking: Attend local events, join community organizations, and engage with local businesses to build connections and establish your presence.

Online Presence: Optimize your website, blog, and social media profiles to showcase your expertise and attract potential clients from different regions.

Virtual Tours: Leverage virtual property tours and online presentations to engage remote buyers and investors interested in properties outside your immediate area.

Client Referrals: Encourage satisfied clients to refer friends, family, or colleagues who may be interested in real estate services in your target locations.

Collaborate with Agents: Partner with agents from different areas to tap into their local networks and offer assistance to clients looking to relocate.

Localized Content: Create content that highlights the benefits of living in various neighborhoods or regions, catering to the interests of potential buyers.

Market Research: Conduct thorough market research in your desired expansion areas to understand local trends, demand, and competition.

Specialized Expertise: Position yourself as an expert in specific niche markets or property types, attracting clients seeking your specialized knowledge.

Engage in Online Forums: Participate in online real estate forums, groups, or platforms to connect with potential clients and share your insights.

Language and Cultural Sensitivity: If targeting international clients, consider learning basic phrases or cultural nuances to enhance your communication.

Localized Advertising: Tailor your advertising efforts to the specific needs and preferences of clients in different regions, showcasing properties and benefits.

Collaborative Marketing: Partner with local businesses, such as moving companies or interior designers, to cross-promote services and expand your reach.

Consistency: Maintain a consistent and active online and offline presence to establish credibility and attract clients from various locations.

By incorporating these strategies, you'll be well-equipped to broaden your client base and extend your geographic reach, effectively positioning yourself as a trusted real estate professional in multiple regions.

Diversifying Income Streams: Investments And Property Management

Diversifying income streams as a real estate agent involves a strategic and forward-thinking approach:

Property Management: Offer property management services to landlords, generating recurring income from managing rental properties.

Real Estate Investments: Invest in real estate properties yourself, generating rental income and potential capital gains over time.

Real Estate Development: Explore real estate development projects, such as building or renovating properties for resale or rental income.

Real Estate Consulting: Provide specialized consulting services, such as market analysis, investment advice, or property valuation, to clients and investors.

Real Estate Education: Host workshops, webinars, or courses to share your expertise with aspiring real estate professionals or property investors.

Real Estate Coaching: Offer coaching services to guide new agents or investors, sharing your knowledge and insights to help them succeed.

Real Estate Syndication: Form investment syndicates where multiple investors pool funds for larger real estate projects, earning a share of profits.

Affiliate Marketing: Partner with companies that offer services relevant to real estate, earning commissions for referrals through your network.

Real Estate Software: Develop or promote software tools tailored for real estate professionals, earning income through licensing or subscriptions.

Flipping Contracts: Engage in wholesaling by contracting to purchase properties at a discounted rate and assigning the contract for a fee.

Commercial Leasing: Venture into commercial real estate by assisting businesses in finding and negotiating leases for office or retail spaces.

Real Estate Auctions: Organize or participate in real estate auctions, earning commissions on successful sales.

Property Staging: Offer staging services to clients, helping them enhance their property's appeal and earning a fee for your expertise.

Ancillary Services: Provide additional services like home inspections, mortgage brokering, or insurance referrals, earning commissions or fees.

By exploring these income diversification avenues, you'll create a more resilient and adaptable real estate business that can thrive across various market conditions and provide multiple streams of revenue.

◆ ◆ ◆

CHAPTER 10:
CONTINUOUS LEARNING
AND GROWTH

Staying Educated In A Dynamic Industry

Staying educated in the dynamic real estate industry requires a commitment to continuous learning and adaptation:

Industry Publications: Subscribe to reputable real estate publications, magazines, and blogs to stay updated on market trends, regulations, and industry insights.

Professional Associations: Join real estate associations such as NAR (National Association of Realtors) for access to educational resources, webinars, and networking events.

Seminars and Workshops: Attend seminars, workshops, and conferences focused on real estate, technology, and emerging trends to broaden your knowledge.

Online Courses: Enroll in online courses or certifications that cover specific areas of interest within the real estate field, enhancing your expertise.

Local Market Insights: Stay informed about local market conditions, property values, and neighborhood developments through research and data analysis.

Networking: Engage with fellow real estate professionals, mentors, and experts to exchange insights, share experiences, and learn from one another.

Mentorship: Seek mentorship from seasoned agents who can provide guidance, share practical knowledge, and offer valuable insights.

Webinars and Podcasts: Tune into webinars and podcasts featuring industry experts discussing relevant topics and providing valuable insights.

Regulatory Updates: Stay informed about changes in real estate regulations, laws, and compliance requirements to ensure you operate within legal boundaries.

Technology Adoption: Embrace technology advancements and platforms that enhance your efficiency, marketing, and client interactions.

Market Research: Regularly conduct market research to understand buyer/seller preferences, emerging neighborhoods, and investment opportunities.

Specialization: Consider specializing in a specific niche within real estate, such as luxury properties or commercial real estate, and invest in in-depth knowledge.

Property Valuation: Stay updated on property valuation techniques, comparative market analysis, and appraisal methodologies.

Client Feedback: Leverage feedback from clients to identify areas for improvement and adjust your approach based on their experiences.

By consistently pursuing these avenues of education and knowledge, you'll position yourself as a well-informed and

Attending Workshops, Conferences, And Seminars

Attending workshops, conferences, and seminars is highly valuable for real estate agents as it offers numerous benefits:

Industry Insights: These events provide the latest trends, market updates, and regulatory changes, keeping agents informed about dynamic industry shifts.

Networking Opportunities: Connecting with fellow professionals, experts, and potential clients fosters valuable relationships and collaborations.

Skill Enhancement: Workshops and seminars offer practical knowledge, strategies, and tools to improve sales, negotiation, marketing, and client management skills.

Professional Growth: Learning from experienced speakers and mentors helps agents refine their expertise and adapt to evolving industry practices.

Innovation Exposure: Conferences showcase emerging technologies, software, and practices that can enhance efficiency and client services.

Market Intelligence: Attending can provide firsthand insights into local and national real estate trends, aiding better decision-making.

Motivation and Inspiration: Engaging with industry leaders and success stories can reignite motivation and inspire agents to strive for excellence.

Continuing Education: Many events offer continuing education credits necessary for maintaining licenses and staying compliant.

Fresh Perspectives: Exposure to diverse ideas and viewpoints challenges agents to think creatively and approach challenges differently.

Awareness of Opportunities: Discover new investment prospects, partnerships, or areas for specialization through exposure to various real estate sectors.

While attendance requires time and investment, the knowledge gained, relationships built, and opportunities discovered can significantly contribute to an agent's professional growth and success in the competitive real estate landscape.

Adapting To Industry Changes And Embracing Innovation

Adapting to industry changes and embracing innovation as a real estate agent involves a proactive and strategic approach:

Continuous Learning: Stay informed about industry trends, technological advancements, and market shifts through workshops, seminars, and online resources.

Open-Mindedness: Cultivate a willingness to explore new ideas, technologies, and practices, even if they challenge traditional methods.

Tech Integration: Embrace technology tools and platforms that enhance efficiency, streamline processes, and improve client interactions.

Networking: Engage with fellow professionals, mentors, and experts to exchange insights, share experiences, and learn from one another.

Market Research: Regularly conduct thorough market research to understand buyer/seller preferences, emerging neighborhoods, and investment opportunities.

Customer-Centric Approach: Prioritize understanding and meeting the evolving needs of clients, tailoring your services to provide exceptional experiences.

Experimentation: Test innovative strategies, whether in marketing, virtual tools, or client engagement, to identify what resonates with your target audience.

Feedback Loop: Seek and embrace feedback from clients, colleagues, and mentors to continuously refine your practices and adapt to changing demands.

Adaptable Strategies: Develop flexible business strategies that can pivot to accommodate shifts in the market, economic conditions, or consumer behavior.

Specialization: Consider specializing in a niche market or area of expertise within real estate, positioning yourself as a go-to resource in that field.

Leadership in Change: Be a leader in embracing change within your office or team, inspiring others to adopt innovative practices.

Evolving Marketing: Utilize digital marketing, social media, and online presence to reach and engage tech-savvy clients effectively.

Anticipate Trends: Stay ahead by anticipating future trends and adopting new practices before they become mainstream in the industry.

Positive Mindset: Approach change with a positive and adaptive mindset, viewing challenges as opportunities for growth and improvement.

By embracing these strategies, real estate agents can proactively navigate industry changes, leverage innovation, and position themselves as forward-thinking professionals capable of thriving in a dynamic real estate landscape.

CONCLUSION

As we conclude our shared exploration within the pages of "From Aspiring Agent to Six-Figure Sensation: Unveiling the Real Estate Success Formula." I want to extend my sincere gratitude for joining me on this enlightening journey. Your commitment to growth and your aspiration to reach the echelons of real estate success are truly commendable.

This book is more than just a collection of strategies; it's a blueprint for crafting a rewarding career and a fulfilling life within the realm of real estate. The principles, insights, and techniques you've encountered throughout these chapters are the cornerstones of achieving not just financial prosperity, but personal and professional fulfillment.

Becoming a six-figure real estate agent transcends sales figures; it signifies your mastery of communication, your skill in building relationships, and your resilience in the face of challenges. As you navigate the intricate pathways of this industry, keep in mind that every transaction, every negotiation, and every interaction is an opportunity to refine your craft.

The journey ahead may hold both triumphs and trials, but armed with the knowledge and wisdom from these pages, you're better equipped to navigate any terrain. Continuously seek growth, stay adaptable to evolving market dynamics, and cultivate your network – for in this dynamic field, relationships are often the bedrock of success.

With the final chapter of this book, you're not concluding your journey; you're embracing a new phase of it. Carry the torch of knowledge you've gained, light your path with determination, and let the fire of ambition guide you forward.

Thank you for entrusting me with a part of your journey. As you embark on your own unique path to six-figure success, remember that your potential is limitless, and your impact on the real estate world is bound to be transformative.

To your ongoing journey of achievement and significance,

Best regards,

Dack Douglas

And as an added bonus, here is a lifetime 10% coupon for any t-shirt purchase. Simply scan the QR code below and apply the code BOOK at checkout.